Papatango Theatre Company presents

The world premiere of the winner of the
2018 Papatango New Writing Prize

THE FUNERAL DIRECTOR

DIRECTOR

by Iman Qureshi

The Funeral Director premiered at Southwark Playhouse on
31 October 2018 produced by Papatango Theatre Company Ltd.

It toured in a co-production between Papatango Theatre Company Ltd
and English Touring Theatre in 2019.

THE FUNERAL DIRECTOR

by Iman Qureshi

Cast in order of speaking

Ayesha	**Aryana Ramkhalawon**
Zeyd	**Maanuv Thiara**
Tom	**Tom Morley**
Janey	**Jessica Clark**

Director	**Hannah Hauer-King**
Set & Costume Designer	**Amy Jane Cook**
Lighting Designer	**Jack Weir**
Sound Designer	**Max Pappenheim**
Producer	**Chris Foxon**
Dramaturg	**George Turvey**
Production Manager	**Ian Taylor for eStage**
Costume Supervisor	**Flora Moyes**
Stage Manager	**Jo Alexander**

Cast and Creative Team

Aryana Ramkhalawon | Ayesha

Aryana is from Lincolnshire and trained at the Guildford School of Acting.

Theatre includes *The Tempest, Swallows and Amazons* and *Much Ado About Nothing* (Storyhouse/Grosvenor Park Rep Company); *The Secret Seven* (Storyhouse); *The Hijabi Monologues* (Bush Theatre); *Ode to Leeds* (Leeds Playhouse); *Glasgow Girls* (National Theatre of Scotland/UK tour); *Merlin* (Nuffield Theatre); *The Secret Garden* (Royal Alexandra Theatre Toronto/Royal Festival Theatre Edinburgh); *Twelve Kali Theatre* (Watermans/Birmingham MAC/Rich Mix); *Half and Half* (Welsh Millennium Centre) and *The Rose and Bulbul* (Kaddam/Pulse Connects).

Television includes *Waterloo Road, Lawless - Drama Matters, Doctors, Crime Stories, Bollywood Carmen* and *Jamillah and Aladdin*.

Maanuv Thiara | Zeyd

Maanuv graduated from Bristol Old Vic Theatre School after which he was part of the Bristol Old Vic's anniversary performance of *King Lear*. Other theatre includes *Hamlet* (West End), *A Passage to India* (Park Theatre) and *Trojan Horse* (Leeds Playhouse/Edinburgh Festival, winner of an Edinburgh Fringe First and the Amnesty Freedom of Expression Award).

Television includes *The Boy with the Top Knot*.

Tom Morley | Tom

Tom trained at LAMDA.

Theatre includes *A Room with a View* (Bath Theatre Royal); *Pitcairn* (Chichester Festival Theatre/UK tour); *This Beautiful Future* (Yard Theatre) and *Five Finger Exercise* (The Print Room).

Film includes *Red Sparrow*.

Television includes *Succession, Holby City, Humans, The Musketeers, Father Brown* and *Downton Abbey*.

Jessica Clark | Janey

Theatre includes *Rotterdam* (Trafalgar Studios/ Theatre503); *The Here and This and Now* (Theatre Royal Plymouth); *Skin a Cat* (Bunker Theatre/Vault Festival); *Romeo and Juliet, Merry Wives of Windsor, The Wind in the Willows, The Secret Garden, Macbeth* and *The Comedy of Errors* (Grosvenor Park Open Air Theatre); *My Dear I Wanted to Tell You* (Soho Theatre); *The School for Scandal* (Park Theatre); *Love's Comedy, The Burglar Who Failed* and *Return to Sender* (Orange Tree Theatre); *Be My Baby* (Derby Theatre); *Wild Horses* (Theatre503) and *Respect* (Birmingham Rep).

Television includes *Versailles* (series regular), *Call the Midwife, Casualty, Silent Witness, Broadside* and *In Search of the Bröntes*.

Iman Qureshi | Playwright

Iman's first full-length play *Speed* was produced by Kali Theatre at the Tristan Bates Theatre and her short play *His and Hers* (Soho Theatre) was produced as part of Tamasha's New Muslim Voices. Her play for young people, *Side Effects*, was performed at Canary Wharf Roof Garden and Poplar Union. Iman has been writer in residence at various schools and her short play *Birthday Begum*, written in residence at Mulberry School for Girls, was performed at Rich Mix and Theatre Royal Stratford East. Iman has also been commissioned or produced by Tamasha Theatre, Purple Moon Drama and the BBC and was a member of Tamasha Playwrights and Soho Theatre Writers' Lab. She was shortlisted for Soho Theatre's Tony Craze Award in 2017.

Hannah Hauer-King | Director

Hannah is artistic director and co-founder of all-female theatre company Damsel Productions. After moving from the US, she started her London directing career acting as Resident AD at Soho Theatre in 2014. She now works as a freelance theatre director, co-founder of Damsel, and a theatre, comedy and cabaret programmer for venue Live At Zedel.

Most recent directing work includes *Fabric, Fury* and *Brute* (Soho Theatre); *Grotty, Alginate* and *Breathe* (Bunker Theatre); *Revolt She Said Revolt Again* (Royal Central School of Speech and Drama); *Clay* (Pleasance Theatre); *Witt 'n Camp* (Edinburgh Fringe, Assembly); *Dry Land* (Jermyn Street Theatre); *Hypernormal* (Vaults Festival) and *Dead Playwright* (Old Red Lion Theatre). Associate/Assistant work includes *Romeo & Juliet* (Shakespeare's Globe), *Radiant Vermin* (Soho Theatre) and *Daytona* (Theatre Royal Haymarket).

Amy Jane Cook | Set & Costume Designer

Amy was the winner of Best Design at the Wales Theatre Awards 2017.

Theatre credits include *Jellyfish* (Bush Theatre); *Not Talking* (Arcola Theatre); *Lava* (Nottingham Playhouse); *Our Blue Heaven* (New Wolsey Theatre); *The Rise and Fall of Little Voice* and *St Nicholas* (Theatr Clwyd); *Insignificance* (Theatr Clwyd/ Langham Place, New York); *Up N Under* (UK tour); *The 8th* (Barbican); *Mydidae* (Soho Theatre/Trafalgar Studios); *66 Books* (Bush Theatre/Westminster Abbey); *Mudlarks* (Bush Theatre/HighTide Festival); *Medea* (Gate Theatre); *65 Miles* and *Once Upon a Time in Wigan* (Hull Truck); *Hamlet* (Young Vic, Maria Theatre); *The Water Engine* (Old Vic Tunnels); *Glory Dazed* (Soho Theatre); *The Mobile Phone Show* (Lyric Hammersmith); *Almost Maine* (Park Theatre); *The Separation* (Project Arts Centre, Dublin/Theatre503); *Where the Mangrove Grows* (Theatre503); *To Dream Again* (Theatr Clwyd/Polka); *The Giant Jam Sandwich* (Polka/UK tour); *Thumbelina's Great Adventure* (Cambridge Arts Centre) and *I (Heart) Peterborough* (Pleasance/UK tour).

Jack Weir | Lighting Designer
Jack trained at Guildhall School of Music and Drama and won the ETC award for Lighting Design in 2014. He is a WhatsOnStage Award and two-time OffWestEnd Award nominee for Best Lighting Designer.

Jack previously worked with Papatango on *Hanna* (Papatango at Arcola Theatre and UK tour). Other recent lighting design credits include *Rain Man* (UK tour); *The Boys in the Band* (Vaudeville Theatre); *Dust* (Trafalgar Studios); *Rothschild & Sons* (Park Theatre); *George's Marvellous Medicine* (Leicester Curve/Rose Theatre/UK tour); *Judy!* (Arts Theatre); *Assata Taught Me* (Gate Theatre); *The Plague* (Arcola Theatre); *Out of Order* (Yvonne Arnaud Theatre/UK tour); *Pray So Hard For You* (Finborough Theatre); *La Ronde* (Bunker Theatre); *Four Play* (Theatre503); *Summer In London* (Theatre Royal Stratford East); *Pyar Actually* (Watford Palace/tour); *Talk Radio* (Old Red Lion Theatre); *Holding The Man, Beautiful Thing, Grindr The Opera* and *Maurice* (Above The Stag); *West Side Story* (Bishopsgate Institute) and *Hunch/Velvet* (Pleasance/Assembly Edinburgh).

Max Pappenheim | Sound Designer
Max previously worked with Papatango on *Coolatully* (Finborough Theatre). Other theatre credits include *The Habit of Art* (York Theatre Royal/Original Theatre); *One For Sorrow* (Royal Court); *The Way of the World* (Donmar Warehouse); *A View from the Bridge, Macbeth* (Tobacco Factory); *Dry Powder, Sex with Strangers, Labyrinth* (Hampstead Theatre); *The Children* (Royal Court/Manhattan Theatre Club); *Humble Boy, The Lottery of Love, Sheppey, Blue/Heart, Little Light, The Distance* (Orange Tree); *Ophelias Zimmer* (Schaubühne, Berlin/Royal Court); *Miss Julie* (Theatre by the Lake/Jermyn Street); *The Gaul* (Hull Truck); *Cookies* (Theatre Royal Haymarket); *Teddy, Fabric, Invincible* (UK tour); *Toast* (Park Theatre/59E59 Theaters, New York); *Jane Wenham* (Out of Joint); *Waiting for Godot* (Sheffield Crucible); *My Eyes Went Dark* (Traverse, Edinburgh); *Cargo* (Arcola Theatre); *Common Wealth* (Almeida Theatre); *Creve Coeur* (Print Room); *Wink* (Theatre503); *Spamalot, The Glass Menagerie* (English Theatre, Frankfurt); *The Cardinal, Kiki's Delivery Service* and *Fiji Land* (Southwark Playhouse); *Mrs Lowry and Son* (Trafalgar Studios), *Martine, Black Jesus* and *Somersaults* (Finborough Theatre) and *The Hotel Plays* (Langham Hotel).

Chris Foxon | Producer
Chris is Executive Director of Papatango. His productions with the company include *Hanna* (Arcola Theatre/national tour); *Trestle* (Papatango New Writing Prize 2017, Southwark Playhouse); *Orca* (Papatango New Writing Prize 2016, Southwark Playhouse); *After Independence* (Arcola Theatre, 2016 Alfred Fagon Audience Award, and BBC Radio 4); *Tomcat* (Papatango New Writing Prize 2015, Southwark Playhouse); *Coolatully* (Papatango New Writing Prize 2014, Finborough Theatre); *Unscorched* (Papatango New Writing Prize 2013, Finborough Theatre) and *Pack* and *Everyday Maps for Everyday Use* (Papatango New Writing Prize 2012, Finborough Theatre). He designed and launched GoWrite, Papatango's specialist participation and engagement programme, and instigated the Resident Playwright scheme.

His other productions include *The Transatlantic Commissions* (Old Vic Theatre); *Donkey Heart* (Old Red Lion Theatre/Trafalgar Studios); *The Fear of Breathing* (Finborough Theatre; transferred in a new production to the Akasaka Red Theatre, Tokyo); *The Keepers of Infinite Space* (Park Theatre); *Happy New* (Trafalgar Studios); *Tejas Verdes* (Edinburgh Festival) and *The Madness of George III* (Oxford Playhouse).

Chris also teaches at the Royal Central School of Speech and Drama and the University of York. He is the co-author of *Being a Playwright: A Career Guide for Writers*, published by Nick Hern Books.

George Turvey | Dramaturg
George co-founded Papatango in 2007 and became the sole Artistic Director in January 2013.

Credits as director include *Hanna* (Arcola Theatre/UK tour); *The Annihilation of Jessie Leadbeater* (Papatango at ALRA); *After Independence* (Papatango at Arcola Theatre, 2016 Alfred Fagon Audience Award, BBC Radio 4); *Leopoldville* (Papatango at Tristan Bates Theatre); and *Angel* (Papatango at Pleasance London and Tristan Bates Theatre).

George trained as an actor at the Academy of Live and Recorded Arts (ALRA) and has appeared on stage and screen throughout the UK and internationally, including the lead roles in the world premiere of Arthur Miller's *No Villain* (Old Red Lion Theatre/Trafalgar Studios) and *Batman Live World Arena Tour*.

As a dramaturg, he has led the development of all of Papatango's productions.

He is the co-author of *Being a Playwright: A Career Guide for Writers*, published by Nick Hern Books.

Ian Taylor for eStage | Production Manager
Ian trained at Guildhall School of Music and Drama.

Founded in 2014, eStage provides theatre and event production services for the entertainment industry through its team of experienced production managers, builders, artists and technicians. For Papatango, productions include *Hanna* (Arcola Theatre/UK tour); *After Independence* (Arcola Theatre) and *Tomcat, Orca* and *Trestle* (Southwark Playhouse). Other theatre includes *New Nigerians, The Plague, Not Talking, The Blue Hour of Natalie Barney, Thebes Land, The Cherry Orchard, The Lower Depths, The Island Nation, Werther, Pelléas et Mélisande* and *Il Tabarro* (Arcola Theatre); *Schism* (Park Theatre); *Giulio Cesare* and *Così fan tutte* (Bury Court Opera); *Diary of a Teenage Girl* (Southwark Playhouse); *The Cutlass Crew, The Price, Deep Waters, The Fizz* and *Eliza and the Swans* (W11 Opera); *L'Agrippina* (The Barber Institute of Fine Arts, University of Birmingham); *Our House* (national tour); *Whisper House* (The Other Palace); *Oedipus Rex* and *L'Enfant et Les Sortilèges* (The Philharmonia Orchestra at Royal Festival Hall); *The Man Who Would Be King, Peter Pan* and *Red Riding Hood* (Greenwich Theatre); *Vanities: The Musical* (Trafalgar Studios); *Who Framed Roger Rabbit?* (Future Cinema) and *Jack and the Beanstalk, Snow White, Cinderella* and *Aladdin* (Upstage Productions).

Flora Moyes | Costume Supervisor
Flora trained at Nottingham Trent University.

Theatre for Papatango includes *Orca* (Southwark Playhouse). Other theatre includes *The Sweet Science of Bruising* (Southwark Playhouse); *F**k You Pay Me* (Assembly Rooms, Edinburgh); *Loose Lips* (Big House Theatre Company); *Misty* (Bush Theatre/Trafalgar Studios); *Acceptance* (Hampstead Theatre); *Fast and Furious Live* (world tour); *Private Lives* (London Classic Theatre); *La Ronde* (Bunker Theatre); *Adding Machine* (Finborough Theatre); *Karagula* (STYX); *Landgirls and French Fancies* (Swank Street Theatre) and *Mrs Hudson's Christmas Corker* (Wilton's Music Hall).

Film includes *The Heresy of Champna.*

Television includes *Britain's Got Talent* (SyCo) and *Clowns* (Hofesh Shechter Company).

Production Acknowledgements

2018 Papatango New Writing Prize Reading Team | **Olu Alakija, Ajjaz Awad-Ibrahin, Florence Bell, Kate Brower, Michael Byrne, Sam Donovan, Yasmin Hafeji, Karis Halsall, Richard Hammarton, Rebecca Hill, Natasha Hyman, Jonny Kelly, Carla Kingham, Alice Kornitzer, Callie Nestleroth, Emily Standring, Naomi Sumner, Roisin Symes, Rosie Wyatt**

Image Design | **Rebecca Pitt**

Image Photography | **Michael Wharley**

Production Photography | **The Other Richard**

Press Representation | **Kate Morley PR**

The Funeral Director was originally developed by Papatango with the following cast: **Taj Atwal, Jaz Deol, Rhys Isaac-Jones** and **Rosie Wyatt**.

Many thanks to our generous supporters: Arts Council England, Austin and Hope Pilkington Trust, Backstage Trust, Boris Karloff Charitable Foundation, Ernest Cook Trust, Garfield Weston Foundation, Golsoncott Foundation, Harold Hyam Wingate Foundation, Mildred Duveen Charitable Trust, Leche Trust, Royal Victoria Hall Foundation and Kathryn Thompson.

We are very grateful to our post-show event partners: Naz and Matt Foundation; Inclusive Mosque Initiative; Hidayah.

The Naz and Matt Foundation tackles homophobia triggered by religious belief to help parents accept their children. Their mission is never to let religion, any religion, come in the way of the unconditional love between parents and their children. The Foundation exists to empower and support LGBTQI (Lesbian, Gay, Bisexual, Transgender, Queer, Questioning and Intersex) individuals, their friends and family to work towards resolving challenges linked to sexuality or gender identity, particularly where religion is heavily influencing the situation. The registered UK charity has won multiple awards for their work building bridges between religious and LGBTQI+ communities.
www.nazandmattfoundation.org

Hidayah is a progressive, volunteer-driven organisation championing and supporting causes in the LGBTQI+ arena. Hidayah is mainly for LGBTQI+ Muslims in the UK and the organisation strives to reach out & connect to as many LGBTQI+ Muslims possible, especially those in need. What started off as a group running in London and Birmingham has now expanded to different cities of the UK, holding monthly meetings in other cities like Leeds, Manchester, Newcastle and Glasgow.
www.hidayahlgbt.co.uk

Launched in 2012, the Inclusive Mosque Initiative creates places of worship for marginalised communities for the practice of inclusive Islamic principles. Founded by Tamsila Tauqir and Dervla Zaynab Shannahan, IMI was created with their experiences of exclusion and those of many others in mind. We host regular Friday prayers, seminars and discussion groups. We aim to create a family-friendly place of worship that welcomes people regardless of their religious belief, race, gender, (dis)ability, sexuality or immigration status.
inclusivemosqueinitiative.org

'Remarkable unearthers of new talent' *Evening Standard*

Papatango was founded to find the best new talent in the UK. We discover and champion new playwrights through free, open application schemes and opportunities.

Our flagship programme is the Papatango New Writing Prize, the UK's only award guaranteeing an emerging playwright a full production, publication, 10% of the gross box office, and an unprecedented £6000 commission for a second play. The Prize is free to enter and assessed anonymously, and all entrants receive personal feedback on their scripts, an unmatched commitment to supporting aspiring playwrights. 1384 entries were received in 2018, meaning the Prize continues to receive more annual submissions than any other UK full-length play award.

Writers discovered through the Prize have received Off West End and RNT Foundation Playwright Awards and BAFTAs, made work with the RSC, BBC, Hampstead Theatre, National Theatre, Out of Joint and other leading organisations, and premiered in over twenty countries.

Papatango also run an annual Resident Playwright scheme, taking an emerging playwright through commissioning, development and production. Our first Resident, May Sumbwanyambe, won the 2016 Alfred Fagon Audience Award for our production of *After Independence*, which we then adapted and produced for BBC Radio Four. Our second Resident, Samantha Potter, won a place on the Channel 4 Playwright's Scheme with our backing and Papatango toured her play *Hanna* nationwide in 2018.

Papatango launched a new arm in summer 2017 called GoWrite. GoWrite delivers an extensive programme of free playwriting opportunities for children and adults nationwide. Children in state schools write their own plays which are then professionally performed and published, while adults take part in workshops, complete six month courses at a variety of regional venues culminating in free public performances, or join fortnightly one-to-one career facilitation services.

GoWrite has delivered face-to-face training for over 2000 budding writers in its first year, with £5000 available in bursaries to enable in-need writers nationwide to access our opportunities.

10% of seats at our productions are donated to charities for young people at risk of exclusion from the arts.

Our first book, *Being A Playwright: A Career Guide for Writers* was published in 2018 by Nick Hern Books and described as 'a phenomenon for playwriting good... a bible for playwrights' by award-winning playwright and academic Steve Waters.

All Papatango's opportunities are free and entered anonymously, encouraging the best new talent regardless of means or connections.

Papatango's motto is simple. All you need is a story.

Papatango are a registered charity. We rely on the generous support of individuals as well as trusts and foundations to deliver our unprecedented and unmatched programme of staging world premieres from brilliant artists who would otherwise go unseen, using the success of our discoveries to inspire grassroots writers that they too can break into theatre.

If you would like to support Papatango or get involved in a particular project, then please email **chris@papatango.co.uk.**

We make a little go a long way.

£10 buys a ticket for an in-need young person

£20 funds the resources for a free writing workshop

£50 provides 25 free playtexts for school libraries

£75 hires space for a day of rehearsals

£100 provides a full costume for a character on stage

£200 enables us to travel to run workshops across the UK

£500 pays for a special performance for a school group

£1000 funds a week of script R&D with actors and writer

£2000 supports a budding writer with a seed commission

£6000 commissions a full script from a new writer

£10,000 pays for a brilliant cast for a month-long show

Every donation makes an enormous difference.

Online
For up-to-date news and opportunities please visit:
www.facebook.com/pages/PapaTango-Theatre-Company/257825071298
www.twitter.com/PapaTangoTC
www.instagram.com/papatangotc/
www.papatango.co.uk

Papatango Theatre Company Ltd is a registered charity and a company limited by guarantee. Registered in England and Wales no. 07365398. Registered Charity no. 1152789.

Artistic Director
George Turvey

Executive Director
Chris Foxon

Funding and Development Manager
Ruth Tosha Mulandi

Resident Playwrights
May Sumbwanyambe
Samantha Potter
Sam Grabiner
Dare Aiyegbayo

Board
David Bond
Sally Cookson
Rachel De-Lahay
Sam Donovan
Nicholas Rogers

Artistic Advisers
Colin Barr
Matt Charman
Tamara Harvey
Catherine Johnson
Dominic Mitchell
Con O'Neil
Tanya Tillett

'Southwark Playhouse churn out arresting productions at a rate of knots' *Time Out*

Southwark Playhouse is all about telling stories and inspiring the next generation of storytellers and theatre makers. It aims to facilitate the work of new and emerging theatre practitioners from early in their creative lives to the start of their professional careers.

Through our schools work we aim to introduce local people at a young age to the possibilities of great drama and the benefits of using theatre skills to facilitate learning. Each year we engage with over 5,000 school pupils through free schools performances and long-term in school curriculum support.

Through our participation programmes we aim to work with all members of our local community in a wide ranging array of creative drama projects that aim to promote cohesion, build confidence and encourage a lifelong appreciation of theatre.

Our theatre programme aims to facilitate and showcase the work of some of the UK's best up and coming talent with a focus on reinterpreting classic plays and contemporary plays of note. Our two atmospheric theatre spaces enable us to offer theatre artists and companies the opportunity to present their first fully realised productions. Over the past 25 years we have produced and presented early productions by many aspiring theatre practitioners many of whom are now enjoying flourishing careers.

'A brand as quirky as it is classy' *The Stage*

For more information about our forthcoming season and to book tickets visit www.southwarkplayhouse.co.uk. You can also support us online by joining our Facebook and Twitter pages.

Staff List

Patrons Sir Michael Caine, Peter Gill OBE, Sir Simon Hughes, Andy Serkis

Board of Trustees Christine D Gagnon, Sarah Hickson, Rodney Pearson, Giles Semper, Kathryn Serkis, Glenn Wellman, Tim Wood (chair)

General Manager	Corinne Beaver
Theatre Manager	Joe Deighan
Assistant Technical & Production Manager	Cat Compson
Assistant Theatre Manager	Sophie Quaile
Technical & Production Manager	Chris Randall
Communications Manager	Susie Safavi
Artistic Director/CEO	Chris Smyrnios
Sales & Box Office Coordinator	Charlotte Spencer
Cleaner	Aklilu Sabew Tebeje
Youth & Community Director	David Workman
Box Office Staff	Rachel Atkinson, Rory Horne

Bar Staff Holly Atkinson, Beth Reilly, Jesus Rodriguez Piay-Veiga, Charlotte Smith, Sarah Teale, Kimberley Turford, Michael van der Put, Alex Webb, Camille Wilhelm.

ETT

English Touring Theatre create theatre of outstanding quality, imagination and ambition; work which interrogates and celebrates contemporary England and reflects the diversity of the nation. We have a singular commitment to touring work both nationally and internationally; enabling audiences everywhere to engage with the world around them.

A STREETCAR NAMED DESIRE
Spring 2018

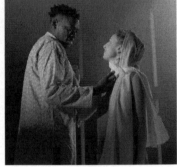

OTHELLO
Autumn 2018

Support text using public funding by
ARTS COUNCIL ENGLAND
LOTTERY FUNDED

ett.org.uk

OUT NOW
THE ESSENTIAL GUIDE
TO A CAREER IN PLAYWRITING

Written by Chris Foxon and George Turvey – the team behind the multi-award-winning Papatango – *Being a Playwright* will help you understand all the practical and business elements of building your writing career.

It includes clear and honest advice on training, getting your script noticed, approaching agents, the development process, working with collaborators, capitalising on a production and more.

Whether you're an aspiring writer wondering how to break into the industry or a working playwright looking to move up to the next level, this book is your road map for navigating the world of professional theatre.

'Packed with inside information that will kick-start your writing life'
Steve Waters, playwright and Senior Lecturer in Creative Writing at the University of East Anglia

'An excellent tool for playwrights navigating today's industry'
Indhu Rubasingham, Artistic Director of Kiln Theatre, London

Available online and in all good bookshops.

THE FUNERAL DIRECTOR

Iman Qureshi

Acknowledgements

This play has been several years in the making, and over those years I have accrued many debts of gratitude. I would like to thank:

My early readers and mentors on Soho Theatre Writers' Lab where this play was conceived. Deirdre O'Halloran who guided *The Funeral Director* through its infancy. Fellow playwrights Holly Robinson and Caitlin McEwan, my go-to agony aunts.

Chris and George at Papatango Theatre. For your enduring belief in this play and colossal efforts to produce it, I am forever indebted. Hannah, for the tenderness, brilliance and love with which you brought it to life. The cast: Aryana, Maanuv, Jess and Tom, for the truth and compassion you gifted these characters, and the enthusiasm, humour and good will that you brought with you every day. The crew: Amy, Max, Jack, Ian, Flora and Jo – whose talents have transformed this play into something that outpaces even my wildest dreams. Taj Atwal, Jaz Deol, Rosie Wyatt and Rhys Isaac-Jones, for uncovering new dimensions and picking holes in early drafts.

Adam Wagner for legal guidance. Haji Taslim Funerals for answering my occasionally uncomfortable questions.

Fin Kennedy and the 'Tamafia' – without you, I'm nothing.

My agent, Alexandra Cory whose punt on me has given me worlds of confidence and, dare I say, hope for an actual career doing what I love.

Southwark Playhouse, Nick Hern Books, and English Touring Theatre.

My colleagues at Shelter, for bearing with me and 'my other job'.

Gareth Lee, Martyn Hall, Steven Preddy and countless others who have fought so courageously for equality, be it loudly in courts of law, or quietly in their homes and communities.

My wonderful family. Though you are far away, I carry you with me. Though I take much for granted, I am more grateful than I have words to say.

And always, PCW.

I.Q.

*To Mama and Abba for their unwavering love,
and to PCW for every second of every day*

6

Characters

AYESHA, *twenty-seven-year-old British Pakistani woman, and funeral director*
ZEYD, *twenty-nine-year-old British Pakistani man, Ayesha's husband and also a funeral director*
JANEY, *twenty-seven-year-old barrister, British, and Ayesha's old schoolfriend*
TOM, *late twenties gay man*

A Note on Costume

Ayesha wears hijab but only when she is in the presence of men who are not her relatives. This would typically be in public spaces – at the hospital, or if a client such as Tom is about to enter the funeral home, she would put her hijab on. In front of just Zeyd, or when she is on her own, or even in front of Janey, she can remove her hijab.

Setting

A small divided town in the Midlands. Predominantly set in a Muslim funeral directors' premises.

Time

January to May 2015.

Music

It is desirable for the actress who plays Ayesha to have some training in classical Indian singing.

A Note on the Text

A forward slash (/) denotes overlapping dialogue or an interruption.

An elipses (…) denotes a trailing off or an incomplete sentence.

Square brackets [ ] denote something that might be said or done, or if left unspoken, the sentiment implied.

This text went to press before the end of rehearsals and so may differ slightly from the play as performed.

ACT ONE

Scene One

A Muslim funeral directors' in a small but racially fraught and divided town in the Midlands – present day.

There's a front room where clients are met, and a back room, where bodies are washed, prepared and viewed before burial.

The directors' serves Muslim clients for Islamic funerals, so there are passages from the Quran displayed on the walls, notably – 'TO HIM WE ALL BELONG AND TO HIM WE ALL RETURN.' However, an effort has been made to make the front room look comforting, with a sofa, rugs and fresh flowers, a kettle, teapot and mugs, and some biscuits laid out. It is a bizarre but not unnatural mix of twee English living room meets small community mosque.

The back room is by contrast white and sterile. There is a shower stall along with a few gurneys and coffins.

AYESHA *is alone, preparing a baby's body in the back room, singing to herself – a song by Mehdi Hasan – 'Duniya Kisi Ke Pyaar Mein'.*

ZEYD *enters with some paperwork.*

ZEYD. That's old-school.

AYESHA. I'm an old soul.

ZEYD. News to me.

AYESHA. Was Mum's favourite. She'd sing it to me when I was little.

ZEYD. You should sing more. I like it.

Pause – ZEYD continues working.

AYESHA. Did you order the kafans?

ZEYD. Not yet.

AYESHA. We're almost out.

ZEYD. I know.

AYESHA (*holding a tiny one up – it's a shroud which wraps the dead bodies*). This is the last one.

ZEYD. No it isn't.

AYESHA. It's the last one in this size.

ZEYD. Well, inshallah we won't get any more babies today.

AYESHA. You better hope we get someone in – this month has been slow.

ZEYD (*blows his hands for warmth*). You think this bloody cold would be killing people off left right and centre.

AYESHA. You could put on the heating.

ZEYD. Alright, big spender.

AYESHA. It'll kill me if you're not careful.

They go back to work.

ZEYD. What do you think she would have been? If she grew up.

AYESHA. I don't know.

ZEYD. I think she would have been a politician.

AYESHA. Doesn't matter now.

ZEYD. She's got this little frown, look? Like she's concentrating. She'd be intelligent. Principled.

AYESHA. Nah, she just grumpy.

ZEYD. She'd be an ambassador for Muslims. Like that Malala. Only not so annoying.

AYESHA. No. She'd be a grumpy waitress. With a grumpy face.

ZEYD. Sure you're not talking about your own face?

Beat.

What's with you today?

AYESHA. Nothing.

Beat.

Babies. She's just a baby.

ZEYD. I told you I could handle this one.

AYESHA. So can I.

ZEYD. It was her time.

AYESHA. Why? Who says? It isn't fair.

ZEYD. We can't question Allah. How he chooses to challenge us. You don't know, maybe this was for the best.

AYESHA. How? How is this for the best?

ZEYD. Maybe she would have grown up to be – Evil. A really bad politician. Like a brown Theresa May.

AYESHA. She had her whole life ahead of her.

ZEYD. This is the life Allah planned for her. Anyway, what life? You want her to be a grumpy waitress.

AYESHA. I guess.

ZEYD. See? Our all knowing Allah has just saved the world from poor service. Some time in the future, someone, somewhere will order a plate of chips. And you know what they'll get?

AYESHA. What?

ZEYD. A plate of chips. And you know why? Because this baby wasn't there to fuck it up.

AYESHA *smiles but then quickly returns to her pensive state and they work in silence.*

Sure you'll be okay on your own if I go to Hamza's stag?

AYESHA. I'll be fine.

ZEYD. Sure? You seem a bit…

AYESHA. I'm fine. Really.

ZEYD. Because I can always…

AYESHA. No. You have a good time. Lads lads lads.

ZEYD. Worried?

AYESHA. About you? Please.

ZEYD. Never know, I might be a catch in Budapest.

AYESHA. Sure.

ZEYD. A dark and handsome prince amongst all those pasty goray.

AYESHA. I'll put an advert in the *Hungarian Times*. One of them what-you-call-its?

ZEYD. Like for-sale ads?

AYESHA. No stupid.

Wracks her brain.

Lonely hearts!

ZEYD (*suddenly hurt that she isn't more jealous*). You could pretend to care a little.

AYESHA. Come on, I trust you. Why would I be worried?

Beat.

So what should we get them?

ZEYD. As a wedding gift?

AYESHA. Yeah.

ZEYD. We just got money for our wedding.

AYESHA. So boring.

ZEYD. It's traditional. I thought you were old-school.

AYESHA. Shut up. Come on we should get them something useful. Like. A kettle.

Beat – realising this is shit.

Like, a really nice kettle.

Beat.

Like one of them ones where you can set the temperature.

Beat.

Okay fine. Money. We just – can't spare much, that's all.
You know that.

ZEYD. Don't worry, he'll understand.

AYESHA *goes back to singing and tidying up.* ZEYD
glances down at the baby.

I want one.

AYESHA. A kettle?

ZEYD. A baby.

AYESHA....

ZEYD. Don't you?

AYESHA. What if it... [dies.]

ZEYD. Inshallah, she won't.

AYESHA. She?

ZEYD. Always wanted a girl.

AYESHA. Well what if she becomes a grumpy waitress and
then dies?

ZEYD. Not all girls have to be waitresses. I thought you were a
feminist. Besides, we won't let that happen.

AYESHA. You can't promise that.

ZEYD. I can. Most babies don't die. Most babies live. Ours
would live. And we'd send her to university. So she won't
be a waitress or a funeral director. She could be anything
she wanted.

AYESHA. Unless she dies.

ZEYD. Well, if she has to die, better she dies a baby, then hey? No memories.

AYESHA. I'll have nine months of memories. What will you have?

ZEYD. So you don't want one at all?

AYESHA. No. Not now anyway.

ZEYD (*silent at first, but then decides to press*). When then?

AYESHA. I don't know. Five years.

ZEYD. We've been married five already. I'm nearly thirty, I don't want to be one of those weird old dads where people think I'm the granddad.

Beat.

My parents are on my case you know. Mum's been knitting baby sweaters for years. And Dad told me to see a doctor if we were 'having problems'.

AYESHA. They should mind their own business.

ZEYD. Grandchildren are their business. And they're worried.

AYESHA. There's no reason to be worried. Tell them we're fine.

Beat.

ZEYD. Aren't you meant to be broody or something? You know, maternal pangs? Don't you get them?

AYESHA. No.

ZEYD *gives up. They work in silence again. Then* ZEYD *tries a different tack.*

ZEYD. Have you read *The Little Prince*?

AYESHA. What?

ZEYD. It's a children's book.

AYESHA. I've never seen you read a book.

ZEYD. Was before we got married.

AYESHA. Oh you've let yourself go have you now? Got no one to impress with your reading?

ZEYD. It's about this guy. Who meets a prince. And the prince tells him stories, becomes his best friend. The guy loves the prince really, but at the end, the prince dies /

AYESHA. Bored to death with his own stories.

ZEYD. No. Listen. You'll miss the point.

AYESHA. Sorry.

ZEYD. The prince tells the guy he's going to die, and the guy is obviously really sad. But the prince says – it's okay. It's okay because when you've stopped grieving you'll remember all the good times we had, and the memories will make you happy.

AYESHA....

ZEYD. What I'm saying is – what I'm saying is – better to love and lose than never /

AYESHA. I know what you're saying.

ZEYD. I know – this job, all we see is the sad stuff. The loss, the death, the worst bits. But there are good bits too. We could have that. And the pain – it's worth it, right?

AYESHA. I've got to go pick Mr Mohajir's body up from the morgue.

Beat.

Can you believe he finally went?

Beat.

Story is he was knocking one off to a Bollywood film, when suddenly – heart attack. Wonder what film it was.

Beat.

You know the rumour right? Apparently he had an implant –
down there.

Beat.

So even though he's gone, his mister will be saluting you on
the table.

Beat.

New one for us hey?

Beat.

ZEYD. Ayesha, I want a family.

The bell in the front room goes and TOM *enters.*

AYESHA. I'll go see.

AYESHA *heads towards the front room and sees it's a white
man –* TOM. *Surprised, she beckons* ZEYD *to come with
her.* TOM *looks distraught.*

(*Whisper to* ZEYD.) It's a gora.

ZEYD *takes charge.*

ZEYD. Hi there, how can I help?

TOM. I need to organise a uh funeral.

ZEYD. Okay.

TOM. A Muslim one.

ZEYD. Right. And who is the deceased?

TOM. My – friend. He's at the hospital. With the coroner – He
just died. He's dead. He's…

ZEYD. Okay, sit down. Here. Ayesha, can you make some tea?

AYESHA *gets up to make some tea.*

Okay, first things first – have you registered the death?

TOM. No they won't let me, say they need to – investigate or
something.

ZEYD. Okay alright, that doesn't take too long usually, okay? Don't worry. So you're not a relative?

TOM. No, he's my – my – friend. He's a Muslim.

ZEYD. Okay, sorry to ask, but did you – did you find the body?

TOM (*nods, nearly in tears*). Yes.

ZEYD. Okay, so when the coroner's done, you'll be able to register the death as you found the body.

TOM. How long does that take? Don't you need to be buried in twenty-four hours? If you're Muslim?

ZEYD. As soon as possible, but you don't worry about that.

TOM. I'm sorry. It's just all so. I don't know what to do. I've never.

ZEYD. You're a good friend, okay? A very good friend for coming here.

TOM. So what do I do then? Once I've registered… Where do I even go to do that?

ZEYD. The coroner will explain everything to you, okay? It'll be okay.

TOM. And the funeral?

ZEYD. So, with arranging the funeral, that's more for the family to do. Different Muslim families do things differently – depending on where they're from, if they're Shia or Sunni.

TOM. He was Sunni, I think. I think so anyway.

ZEYD. Okay, well, do you have his family's contact details? It's just so we can be in touch with them, see what arrangements they'd like.

TOM. I was practically family.

ZEYD. Okay…

TOM. He was my flatmate. We were close. I know what sort of arrangements he'd like.

ZEYD. It's just – we always deal with family, we need to make sure that everyone is involved

TOM. They don't want to be involved.

ZEYD. What do you mean?

TOM. I mean, he didn't speak to his family.

ZEYD. I'm sure they'll want to know their son has died...
Arrange a funeral for him.

TOM. They know, they know he's died. They just – don't want to have anything to do with him.

Pause. AYESHA *has clocked what's going on and looks at* ZEYD *pointedly. She puts a cup of tea down in front of* TOM.

ZEYD. Your friend – is he local?

TOM. Yes. Up the road. Cheevely Avenue.

ZEYD *and* AYESHA *glance at each other.* ZEYD *realises something's not right now too, but isn't sure quite what.*

ZEYD. How did he – uh. How did he die?

TOM. What's that got to do with anything?

ZEYD. Well, he must be a young lad, your age. And if they suspect it's a [suicide]... /

TOM. It was an accident. An accident. He didn't mean to do it. Just wanted to scare them. He took pills. Too many pills and they tried to pump his – they couldn't, there were too many and it was too late. We were happy though. We were, I know it. He couldn't have meant it.

ZEYD *has now realised what's going on.*

AYESHA. I'm sorry we can't help you.

TOM. What?

AYESHA. We're too busy at the moment.

TOM. But surely you're used to being busy. Surely you could... /

AYESHA. It's been a cold winter. A lot of the elderly have passed away recently. We just can't manage with another.

TOM. Please. I don't know where else to go, who else to speak to.

AYESHA. Sorry.

TOM. Sorry!?

ZEYD. What's your name, mate?

TOM. Tom.

ZEYD. Listen, Tom. Why don't you go to Freddy's. Frederick and Sons, other side of town. You know it? They'll sort it. They're really good up there.

TOM. But I came here because he was Muslim.

ZEYD. We'll give Freddy's a call. Tell them how to do it.

TOM. What? Why can't you just do it?

ZEYD. Sorry. If I'm honest, we've just got too many clients around these parts /

AYESHA. We're all booked up.

TOM. Please. He would have wanted it done the Muslim way. I don't even know what that is, but I know – it was important to him.

AYESHA. I'm really sorry.

TOM. Thanks anyway.

TOM *looks defeated, turns and leaves.*

ZEYD. Poor boy.

AYESHA. It was the right decision.

ZEYD. I know. I just wish we could have helped.

AYESHA. But the family…

ZEYD. I know.

AYESHA. There's no way.

ZEYD. I wish we could have done it quietly.

AYESHA. Nothing stays quiet in this town.

ZEYD. Do you think we could have spoken to the imam?

AYESHA. And said what? He'll know the parents.

ZEYD. I know.

AYESHA. This is my mum's business. I need to run it the way she…

ZEYD. I know.

AYESHA. And she wouldn't have wanted…

ZEYD. I know.

AYESHA. You keep saying you know but you don't sound like you do.

ZEYD.…

AYESHA. I'm going to the hospital. See you later.

Beat.

Order those kafans.

AYESHA *leaves.*

Scene Two

The hospital.

AYESHA *is waiting at a reception desk.* JANEY, *tired, puffy-eyed, is carrying two cups of tea back from the vending machine.* JANEY *recognises* AYESHA *instantly, but* AYESHA *is taken by surprise.*

JANEY. Oh my god – Ayesha??

AYESHA. Janey. What are you…

JANEY *hurries over to* AYESHA, *possibly with the intention to hug her awkwardly. But in the process of this,* JANEY *spills tea over her hands, eliminating any opportunity for a hug.*

JANEY. Ow… FUCK! Why do they always make that machine tea so bloody hot?

She blows on her own hand while AYESHA *looks on helplessly.*

This is a hospital! You'd think the last thing they'd want is to scald their patients.

AYESHA. Sorry.

JANEY. It's fine, really. It's fine. Skin grows back, doesn't it?

AYESHA. Do you want me to – get you another?

JANEY. No it's okay, I was taking it for Mum. She can just have this.

JANEY *decants one tea into what remains of the other.*

I've had enough caffeine for one night anyway.

AYESHA. Your mum's in here?

JANEY. Yes. Most likely just doing some attention-seeking again.

Beat.

She was up a ladder. Trimming the neighbour's hedge. They didn't ask her to. She just – took it upon herself. Classic move from the mothership really. But she slipped, fell. Miraculously, no broken bones, just a sharp whack on the head.

An awkward beat.

I think she's fine. Just a scare.

AYESHA. Good. So you're back?

JANEY. Oh no. God no. Came up last night. Wanted to earlier, soon as I'd heard, but work and stuff. So got the last train up, and I've been at the hospital since. I probably look a right state.

AYESHA. No. You don't.

JANEY. Well, I feel rough.

Beat.

It's been ages since I last saw you /

AYESHA. Eleven years /

JANEY. Eleven years.

Beat.

And I'm a lawyer now. In London.

AYESHA (*impressed*). Oh.

JANEY. Feels like the other side of the world sometimes, but it's only a couple of hours away I guess.

AYESHA. Your mum's still…

JANEY. Here yeah. I should visit her more. You think they'll always be there, don't you? Mums. When you need them. Then something like this – reminds you, they won't be.

AYESHA. Well, she's alright now. That's the main thing.

JANEY. Yeah.

Beat.

AYESHA. It was nice to see you.

AYESHA*'s wrapping it up.*

JANEY. Wait – I didn't even… Sorry I'm so tired, I've been up all night, and Mum is – difficult. As ever. Sure you remember. So I'm just feeling a bit. But I didn't even ask about you. Or anything. What are you doing here?

AYESHA. I live here.

JANEY. In hospital.

AYESHA. No obviously not in hospital /

JANEY. No I mean what are you doing in hospital. Are you okay?

AYESHA. Oh, I'm fine, it's just work.

JANEY. Are you a doctor now?

AYESHA. No – Uhm. The funeral home.

JANEY….

AYESHA. I'm collecting someone?

JANEY. Oh. Of course – people die in a hospital, Janey. You idiot.

Beat.

AYESHA. Your mum will be fine.

JANEY. Sure. Yes. She will. She's a tough old boot, isn't she. She'll never let me get rid of her that easily.

Beat.

How is the funeral home? Same place is it?

AYESHA. Yeah

JANEY. And your mum?

AYESHA. She – died.

JANEY (*visibly stunned*). Oh! I didn't know…

AYESHA. Why would you?

JANEY. When?

AYESHA. Few years ago.

JANEY. You should have told me. Here I am banging on about my mum and... You should have told me. I'd have come. To the funeral...

AYESHA. It was all a bit of a blur...

JANEY. Course.

Beat.

I'm so sorry, Ayesha.

AYESHA. It's okay. Nothing like being a funeral director to prepare you for death.

JANEY *smiles.*

JANEY. I've missed you.

Beat.

AYESHA. I married Zeyd.

Beat.

JANEY. Course. Course you did.

AYESHA. Are you – you married?

JANEY. No, nope. Single. [Ready to mingle.]

JANEY*'s phone rings. She juggles the cups of tea and pulls it out but doesn't pick it up.*

It's Mum. I'm surprised it took her this long to ring.

Beat.

Look I'd better be off. She hates being in here. Machine tea and foreign doctors – don't know which she trusts least.

Beat.

Sorry. Look I'd love to see you again. Properly? Once I know what's happening... with Mum and all?

AYESHA. Well, work is always busy.

JANEY. Surely you get a day off.

AYESHA. People can die any time. We're always on-call.

JANEY. Surely someone will be kind enough to put off their
dying for a day or so?

AYESHA. I don't think it's a good idea.

Beat.

JANEY. Okay. Well. Good to see you then. Glad you're doing –
alright. I'll be staying at Mum's for a few weeks at least.
Same landline number, believe it or not, if you change your
mind. Well. Anyway. See you around. Maybe.

AYESHA *watches* JANEY *go.*

Lights down.

Scene Three

In the funeral home, front room.

ZEYD *enters in a suit looking dashing, with a wrapped present
and a bunch of flowers. He looks frantically around, trying to
find a place to conceal the present. He's interrupted by*
AYESHA*'s keys in the door. Panicking, he stuffs the present
behind a cushion on the sofa.*

AYESHA *enters with some letters, reading a card in her hand.*

ZEYD. Happy birthday!

AYESHA. Why are you so dressed up?

ZEYD *holds out a bunch of flowers, but she is distracted by
the card.*

ZEYD. What's that?

AYESHA. It's from Janey, remember my friend from school?

ZEYD. Yeah.

AYESHA. Can't believe she remembered.

ZEYD. She sent you a birthday card out the blue?

AYESHA. I bumped into her in hospital a few weeks ago. Her mum had an accident.

ZEYD. Oh. She living back here now??

AYESHA. London. She's a lawyer.

ZEYD. Well. Good for her.

Beat.

I got you flowers. For your birthday.

AYESHA. Aren't these from yesterday's funeral?

ZEYD. No...

AYESHA. Yes they are!

ZEYD. Well, I didn't want to waste them.

AYESHA. You charmer.

ZEYD. That's not all. There's more!

AYESHA. More than leftover funeral flowers. Lucky me!

ZEYD. I've booked us dinner. Nice restaurant, candles...

AYESHA. Oh... I need to sort some burial forms...

ZEYD. I can do that, if you want to get ready?

AYESHA. Well, who's going to be on-call?

ZEYD. I've asked Hamza.

AYESHA *looks at* ZEYD *properly.*

AYESHA. Forgiven you for missing his stag, has he?

Beat.

You look nice.

ZEYD. Come here.

He opens his arms out to her. They hug, he kisses her head or cheek – somewhere platonic.

AYESHA. You smell nice.

ZEYD. You too. I mean, you smell a bit of formaldehyde, but that's okay.

AYESHA. Idiot. The Rahmans wanted their mum repatriated so I had to embalm.

ZEYD. To Bangladesh?

AYESHA *nods, tiredly.*

Why? They all live here?

AYESHA. Her wishes.

ZEYD. She was British!

AYESHA. I don't know, Zeyd. Maybe this miserable weather?

ZEYD. Weather makes no difference six feet under.

AYESHA *notices the misplaced cushions.*

AYESHA. This place is a mess.

ZEYD *sees her going to straighten the cushions, intervenes…*

ZEYD. No don't!

(*More calmly.*) You just leave that to me. You should go shower, get changed, and then we're going for dinner, okay?

AYESHA (*noticing something behind the cushion*). What's that?

ZEYD. What? Nothing.

AYESHA. I can see you're hiding something.

ZEYD. It's nothing

AYESHA. If it's nothing, let me see.

ZEYD. I need to return it. I ordered it by mistake.

AYESHA. What is it?

ZEYD. Nothing!

AYESHA. Why are you being so weird?

ZEYD. Why are you being so nosy?

AYESHA. Because you're being weird!

ZEYD. It was a present for you okay, but – they sent the wrong um size.

AYESHA (*pleased, surprised*). Oh! What is it, shoes? Why don't you show me anyway?

ZEYD. Uh – it's not shoes.

AYESHA. Then what?

ZEYD. Something else.

AYESHA. Why are you being so weird then? Come on show me!

ZEYD. No!

AYESHA. It's my birthday!

AYESHA begins to tickle him playfully, and he can't handle it. ZEYD *cracks and hands her a gift.*

You wrapped it and everything.

She unwraps it and sees what it is – a huge vibrator.

Is this a joke?

ZEYD. It was meant to be – in the photos it looked – Um. Smaller. Not as uh… veiny.

AYESHA. Why – uh – why…

ZEYD. The Amazon reviews were all five star and…

AYESHA. You got this on Amazon?

ZEYD. Did you know, they do next-day delivery now. Isn't that good?

AYESHA. Do you know what this is?

ZEYD. I'm not a complete idiot.

AYESHA. I don't know what to say…

ZEYD. You don't need to be embarrassed or – hey, we're married and, you know it's halal and all, so you don't need to…

AYESHA. I'm not, I just don't understand…

ZEYD. I thought we could – maybe…

AYESHA. Maybe?

ZEYD. We could maybe try for a baby.

AYESHA. With this?

ZEYD. I know, I know. I just thought it might – because we don't – we haven't in a long time.

AYESHA. Right. And this?

ZEYD. For you – to use.

AYESHA. On you or me?

ZEYD. No, no – not on me. On you.

AYESHA. I'm sorry I can't – can you just hold it please.

ZEYD takes it in his hands gingerly, while AYESHA shakes her hands out and begins to pace the room.

ZEYD. I just thought – we could – you could – try it. You know, by yourself, or with me, maybe? Or maybe even if I could just – watch?

AYESHA. Watch?

ZEYD. Watch.

AYESHA. You want to watch me. Use that. So we can have a baby.

ZEYD. Exactly. Is that weird?

AYESHA. Yes. Mainly because that isn't how babies are made.

ZEYD. But I want you to enjoy it. Because I don't think you do.

Beat.

I've been listening to this podcast. Sex advice.

AYESHA. Oh good.

ZEYD. And I realised we never really talk about it. Sex. I mean maybe it's because we never do it.

AYESHA. Not never.

ZEYD. Hardly ever. And when we do – I can tell, you just want it to be over.

Beat.

And I just thought – well, because it said that women reach their sexual peak in their late twenties, so maybe now you're twenty-eight, you'll, you know, peak?

AYESHA. Peak?!

ZEYD. Yes. Peak. And maybe you'll enjoy it. And then we could try for a baby.

AYESHA. And you thought my birthday was a good time to bring this up?

ZEYD. I just want you to be happy.

AYESHA. I am happy.

ZEYD. You are?

AYESHA. Yes.

ZEYD. Without – you know. Sex?

AYESHA. Yes.

ZEYD. You're happy without sex?

AYESHA. Is that wrong?

ZEYD. No, it's just – the thing is – I don't think I'm – I'm not happy. Without it. Without sex.

AYESHA. So maybe you need that. I hope you two live happily ever after.

ZEYD. This isn't funny. We're married. And – and I love you, so what's so wrong with…

AYESHA. And this is my birthday. I can't believe we're talking about this on my birthday.

ZEYD. Well when should I bring it up?

AYESHA. I don't know, Zeyd. We work together, live together. You have three hundred and sixty-four other days to choose from. Take your pick. Maybe on your fucking birthday if you want to talk about it so badly.

ZEYD. I hate it when you swear.

AYESHA. Well I hate it when you give me a rubber penis for my birthday.

ZEYD. It's silicone. I did all the research. It's the best one.

AYESHA. Oh how considerate.

ZEYD. Well – it's non-refundable, so –

Beat.

You wanna keep it anyway?

AYESHA. No! Use it yourself or throw it away, I don't care. Just get it away from me.

ZEYD *examines it forlornly. This has not gone to plan.*

Beat.

ZEYD. We're going to be late for dinner. You've still got time to change first though, if you want?

AYESHA. I don't really feel like changing. Or dinner actually.

ZEYD *looks heartbroken.*

ZEYD. No. That's okay. Whatever you want, love.

AYESHA *returns to the pile of post she brought in with her, opening a few letters, glancing at them, putting them to one side.*

I'm sorry.

Beat.

I didn't mean to upset you.

Beat.

I know I shouldn't have – Maybe it wasn't the best – It's just, that sometimes I just feel like – we're on different – pages or planets, or something.

Long pause. AYESHA *is reading a letter. She puts it down.*

AYESHA. We're being sued.

ZEYD. What?

AYESHA. Thomas Gibbs.

ZEYD. Who?

AYESHA. That boy.

ZEYD. Which boy?

AYESHA. The one we sent away. Ages ago. Remember?

ZEYD. What's he suing us for?

AYESHA. Discrimination. Did you know it was illegal? To turn him away?

ZEYD. What? How?

AYESHA. He says he was discriminated against because of his sexuality.

ZEYD. We didn't say that was why, did we? We didn't say anything about that.

Beat – then snatching the letter from her.

Show me that.

ZEYD *looks at it but briefly, not taking in the detail.*

AYESHA. What have we done?

ZEYD. Hey look, it'll be okay. It's what your mum would have done, right?

AYESHA. I don't know and I can't ask her because she's not here.

ZEYD. This is so messed up. He went to Freddy's anyway, it was all fine. He had the funeral.

AYESHA. How do you know that?

ZEYD. Because I rang them. Told them how to do an Islamic funeral, how to give him the proper ghusl and everything. They sorted it and he got what he wanted so I don't know what the problem is!

AYESHA. I can't believe you did that.

ZEYD. I can't believe he's suing us!

Beat.

Ahad Ilyas.

AYESHA. What?

ZEYD. That boy's name. The one who died. His name was Ahad.

Beat – they acknowledge the impact of what they have done. ZEYD *looks at the card from* JANEY *that* AYESHA*'s put up.*

Your friend from school, the lawyer. She was always round here back then, I remember. Call her, she'll help you.

AYESHA. I don't know her that well any more.

ZEYD. So? Just call and see what she says. Maybe she'll understand.

Beat.

She sent you a birthday card! She obviously cares about you.

AYESHA....

ZEYD (*handing her his phone*). Do you have her number?

AYESHA. Okay, okay, I'll think about it.

Beat.

I can't believe you went to Freddy's to help him. And now he's doing this to us. Why did you bother?

ZEYD. Well, he was so – I could imagine it, you know? How
he felt. I could see it in his face. I'd be like him too, if it was
you who'd died.

Beat.

AYESHA. What will we do?

ZEYD. It'll be okay, love. I promise.

ZEYD *puts his arms around* AYESHA, *tight.*

End of Act One.

ACT TWO

Scene One

Lights up. In the funeral home. JANEY *and* AYESHA *have just been out for a coffee, and return together.*

JANEY. Wow! Look at this place! It hasn't changed one bit!

Beat.

The custard creams! I genuinely haven't eaten a custard cream since I was sixteen.

AYESHA. Do you only eat posh London biscuits now?

JANEY. Oh yeah, each biscuit costs at least six pounds.

AYESHA. Well you better stock up.

AYESHA *offers her a biscuit.*

Go on, have another.

They chomp on biscuits for a moment. JANEY *sees a photo of* ZEYD *and* AYESHA *on the wall.*

JANEY. I still can't believe you married Mr Bum Fluff.

(*Giggles.*) Does he know we used to call him that?

AYESHA. No, and I want it to stay that way!

JANEY. I knew he liked you! Always hanging around you.

AYESHA. Stop!

JANEY. Fine. I just think it's funny, that's all. I should have known you'd end up together.

AYESHA. What's that supposed to mean?

JANEY. Nothing. I just should have guessed.

Beat.

AYESHA. Are you still in touch with anyone?

JANEY. From St Marks, hah, no. Are you?

AYESHA. Well most of them all still live round here.

JANEY. Right. I had a clean break I guess.

Beat – she left AYESHA *behind too.*

AYESHA. Fresh start. Lucky.

Beat.

JANEY. So you going to give me a tour of the back or what?

AYESHA. You still want to see it? You're so weird.

JANEY. You promised!

AYESHA. It isn't special… it's just – imagine a regular room – four walls, tiled. A sink. That's it.

JANEY. Oh come on! I'm dying to see it! Your mum never let us in there!

AYESHA. I know. The more she tried to keep the dead bodies from me, the more curious I was!

JANEY. Guess she just wanted to give you a normal upbringing. Without nightmares of corpses.

AYESHA *(laughing)*. It was a nightmare anyway! You were the only person mental enough to come visit! Everyone else thought our house was haunted! Remember?

JANEY. Oh I thought it was haunted too. That's why it was so exciting!

Beat.

Do you still live upstairs? With Zeyd?

AYESHA. Yeah.

Beat.

I want to move. Fresh start and all. But money's tight and Mum left us the flat. And we can't rent it out because – well who would want to rent a flat above a funeral directors'.

JANEY. You never know. Come on then, let me see the back room.

AYESHA. It's – private.

JANEY. So, it's just me.

AYESHA. I don't know if Zeyd would be okay with it.

JANEY. He's not the boss of you.

AYESHA. I know that.

JANEY. So what's the problem? Is there anyone in there? Dead, I mean.

AYESHA. No, but…

JANEY. Well then! Don't you own this place anyway? You make the rules!

AYESHA. Fine.

JANEY. Yes!

> AYESHA *leads* JANEY *into the back room and flicks the lights on.*

Wow. This is – dull?

AYESHA. What did you expect?

JANEY. Dunno. Bit more. Drama or something.

AYESHA. Sorry to disappoint you.

JANEY. I've never seen a dead body you know.

AYESHA. You're lucky.

JANEY. Guess so. Are you used to it?

AYESHA. No.

> *Beat.*

How's your mum?

JANEY. Out of the woods. But I feel like I should stay. Get to know her again, properly. As adults. But that woman – she's…

AYESHA. I remember.

JANEY. Right. Course.

A beat – something in the past is being referenced but we're not sure what.

I'm sorry I never got in touch. After I left.

AYESHA. It's fine.

JANEY. Are you still singing?

AYESHA. Not really.

JANEY. You were so talented. Why'd you stop?

AYESHA. Grew up, I guess.

JANEY. Remember we'd be in choir together? You'd get all the solos, and I'd stand at the back wailing like a cat on heat.

AYESHA. You were alright.

JANEY. I was awful! I was only there because I wanted to hang out with you!

Beat.

I always thought you were going to be like a singer or something. Never saw you doing this, for some reason.

Beat.

Come on, sing me something…

AYESHA. No, I can't.

JANEY. Yes you can.

AYESHA. It'd be weird.

JANEY. Why? Come on, serenade me… serenade me!

JANEY hops onto a free gurney and poses inappropriately.

AYESHA laughs.

Come on, I'm serious!

AYESHA. You really haven't changed one bit!

JANEY. Is that a bad thing?

AYESHA. No.

Beat.

Have I changed?

JANEY. Yes.

AYESHA. How?

JANEY. Well.

JANEY *sits up on the gurney and touches* AYESHA'*s hijab – it is intimate, perhaps a first touch for them.*

This for one.

Beat.

And I don't know – you're just more serious. Grown up.

Beat.

And maybe – you seem a bit...

AYESHA. A bit what?

JANEY. I don't know...

AYESHA. What?

JANEY. I don't want to say...

AYESHA. What?

JANEY. Maybe... Sad?

AYESHA. Sad?

JANEY. Sad. Yes.

A silence – AYESHA *realises that* JANEY *isn't wrong.*

JANEY *lies back down on the gurney.*

What do you think being dead is like?

AYESHA. Well, we were taught, if you've been good in life –
it's meant to be alright. But if you've been bad, sinful, we
call it 'the torment of the grave'. Your grave, it closes in on
you, and it's full of spiders and beetles and horrible stuff and
it's the longest wait till the Day of Judgement. Even the
animals can hear your screams.

JANEY. And people say atheists are bleak.

AYESHA. Depends on your perspective I guess.

JANEY. What happens on the Day of Judgement then?

AYESHA. Sentenced – to heaven or hell.

JANEY. Is that what you believe?

AYESHA. Yes.

Beat.

I don't know any more. What do you think?

JANEY. I think you're just gone.

AYESHA. I guess, for the people left behind, you are.

JANEY. You must miss her.

AYESHA. Every day.

JANEY. How did she… [die?]

AYESHA. Car accident.

JANEY. That's awful. I'm sorry.

AYESHA. The worst thing was – I'd seen her in here so many
times. Living, breathing, humming to herself as she cared for
all the people who came in over the years. But seeing her in
here – not just dead but mangled.

Beat.

I couldn't wash her – what was left of her. All the bodies I'd
washed, that we'd washed together, and I couldn't wash hers.
Zeyd did it in the end.

JANEY. I thought about her a lot. She was always so lovely to me. Welcoming. The opposite of my mum.

Beat.

I'm sorry about how we left things, you know? Back then. About how my mum dealt with it? The bullying.

AYESHA. It was a long time ago.

JANEY. I'm really sorry.

AYESHA. It's in the past.

Beat.

And we ended up fine.

JANEY. I suppose so.

AYESHA. More than fine! You're a lawyer!

JANEY. A barrister, so the underpaid kind.

AYESHA. What sorts of cases do you do?

JANEY. Human rights, criminal justice, some of the terror cases...

AYESHA. So you defend them? The terrorists.

JANEY. Well they're not proven terrorists but often they've been unlawfully detained. Other times they're tried in what's called secret courts, supposedly for reasons pertaining to national security, but really can anyone actually have a fair trial if it happens in secret, and the government pushed this legislation through despite /

AYESHA. Janey?

JANEY. Yeah?

AYESHA. I need a favour.

JANEY. Oh. Okay.

Beat.

AYESHA. Zeyd and I, we're being sued.

JANEY. What for?

AYESHA. Well. This boy. He came in here a few weeks ago.

JANEY. Right...

AYESHA. He was – younger than most people who come in to bury their wives or children. So I thought it must be his parent who'd died. A convert parent or something, because he was white, and well, why else would there be a white man in a Muslim funeral directors'.

Beat.

And he says – he says his friend's died. Committed suicide we think. And his friend's a Muslim, but didn't speak to his family any more, so this English boy wants to arrange the funeral.

Beat.

Anyway, the dead boy well he's from the community, people would talk, gossip, and because of his reputation we'd be blacklisted. Our business would suffer. We're already up against it.

Beat.

So I say sorry, turn him away. Zeyd sends him to Freddy's Funerals, other side of town.

And then Zeyd even goes to Freddy's. Tells him how to do a Muslim funeral. The rituals and all, so the boy gets what he wants anyway, just not from us.

JANEY. Right. So?

AYESHA. Well, now he's suing us!

JANEY. I don't understand, why?

AYESHA. Discrimination.

JANEY. Well why did you turn him away? What was his reputation?

AYESHA. Well, it must have been his – his boyfriend.

Beat.

We don't know what to do. I thought because you're a lawyer you could help?

Beat.

Say something.

Long pause.

JANEY. I wanted a bit of a break from law, actually.

Beat.

It's partly why I decided to stay up here so long.

AYESHA. So you won't help?

JANEY. I'm sorry, I can't.

AYESHA. Just some advice, anything. We don't know what to do – we can't afford a settlement, and we can't afford a lawyer, and we definitely can't afford to lose the case.

JANEY. This isn't even my area really.

AYESHA. We don't have anyone else.

JANEY. I think I'd better go. Say hi to Zeyd. It was nice of him to go to Freddy's. Terrible to turn the guy away. But nice to do what he did.

AYESHA. Janey.

JANEY. I'm sorry but I really can't help with this. Anything but this.

AYESHA. Please.

JANEY. Bye, Ayesha.

JANEY *leaves.*

Scene Two

In the funeral home – front room. Music is playing in the background – something like 'Aaja' by Swet Shop Boys. AYESHA is cleaning with a broom or mop, and begins to sing/rap along to the song. As she gets more into the song, she starts to dance with the broom.

ZEYD *enters but* AYESHA *doesn't notice.*

ZEYD. Ayesha? Ayesha! AYESHA!!!

　AYESHA *cannot hear him.*

　What's this – song?

　He clearly hates it.

　AYESHA *notices him and jumps, surprised and perhaps a touch embarrassed. She turns the music down.*

AYESHA. What are you doing creeping around?

ZEYD. What are you doing dancing around? Anyone could just walk in!

AYESHA. Was just – cleaning. Anyway we're closing up now.

　Pause.

ZEYD. You seem happier.

AYESHA. Guess so.

ZEYD. Good to have the imam on side, isn't it.

AYESHA. Yeah.

ZEYD. Nice to hear you sing again. Dancing could use a bit of work though.

AYESHA. Oi.

ZEYD. It's okay. Maybe we could get dancing lessons together.

　He reaches for her and dances with her a bit unsteadily.

AYESHA. As if we have time.

ZEYD. We could hire someone to help.

AYESHA. You need a woman for the female ghusls.

ZEYD. So we'll hire a woman.

AYESHA. Good luck finding one.

ZEYD. We'll make it work.

They continue to dance.

You should record some songs, you know. Put them on
YouTube or something.

AYESHA. No.

ZEYD. I'm serious. You're really talented. You could be
something. Maybe you could get some lessons. Do a course.

AYESHA. Don't be stupid.

ZEYD. I'm not! You know when I told them over at Freddy's
how to do an Islamic funeral, part of me just thought, that's
it. Let's pack it in. Freddy's can do them. Let's go do
something we actually want to do! We're so young, you
inherited this business. You weren't even given a choice.

AYESHA. This is my choice. It's my mum's business and
I choose to keep it going for her.

ZEYD. So we can always come back to it. But for a few years,
you could… sing? Take lessons, perform? I could – I don't
know. Do other stuff. Anything. We've been working our
guts over this place I don't even have time for hobbies or
friends or anything. Running this business has become all we
do. Let someone else do it.

AYESHA. What is with you?

ZEYD. Look I'm not saying throw it all away. All I'm saying is,
you're talented, and it makes you happy. So do it. And we'll
make everything else work. We spend all our days burying
the past. Let's think about the future for a change.

Pause.

AYESHA. How did I get so lucky?

ZEYD. Lucky?

AYESHA. With you.

ZEYD. Oh.

Pause.

AYESHA. When Mum first tried to set us up, I was only eighteen, you know. I thought she was mad. I'd never looked at you like that. The hearse-driver boy. The errand boy. The boy who, try as he might, couldn't grow a beard.

ZEYD. Oi!

AYESHA. But she kept saying, he's a good boy, he'll be understanding, he'll be gentle. After my dad, I guess she could spot the bastards a mile off. And she knew you weren't one of them.

Beat.

I wish she could have seen us married.

ZEYD. Me too.

AYESHA. It would have made her so happy. She would have seen that you're not just good, you're the best. Not just understanding but patient and kind too.

AYESHA *touches* ZEYD*'s shirt buttons, flirtatiously. He beams.*

I was thinking.

ZEYD. Yeah?

AYESHA. About what you said. About a family?

ZEYD. Yeah?

AYESHA. And how we're surrounded by death, so we should bring something new into the world.

ZEYD. Yes! Exactly! That's what I was trying to say /

AYESHA kisses ZEYD on the lips. ZEYD is beyond delighted but is nervous – she never initiates sex. From now on, ZEYD is trying to seduce AYESHA but very tentatively, so as not to ruin the moment. AYESHA is trying to get herself there too, but is struggling, delaying, asking questions, which ZEYD is trying to bat off so they can get to the sex.

AYESHA. So you want a girl.

ZEYD. Yeah but I'm not fussy.

AYESHA. Why a girl?

ZEYD. Just always how I imagined it. As a dad with three little girls.

AYESHA. Three! Allah!

ZEYD. Better make a start huh?

AYESHA. Why not boys?

ZEYD. What?

AYESHA. Why don't you want sons?

ZEYD. Sure sons are fine.

AYESHA. Boys are easier, aren't they?

ZEYD. For who?

AYESHA. Everyone. Don't need to worry about them so much. Life's harder for girls.

ZEYD. How?

AYESHA. You saw how my mum suffered? Being a divorced woman, a single parent. Raising me, running a business – running THIS business. I don't want that for my daughter.

ZEYD. We'll raise her proper though.

Beat.

Why are we talking about this? You know I read that this is called 'catastrophising'.

AYESHA. Oh reading again, are we.

ZEYD. Yeah. It means always thinking that something bad will happen. Everything will be fine. Come here…

ZEYD kisses AYESHA, *attempts to rekindle their earlier romance. She receives the kiss for a moment before pulling away to say…*

AYESHA. If you had a girl, would you force her to dress Islamically?

ZEYD. I don't know. I guess maybe not force her, but encourage.

AYESHA. Why?

ZEYD. Well, otherwise, how will she know who we are? Her identity?

AYESHA. She can make her own identity.

ZEYD. No we have to teach her.

AYESHA. Well would you make a boy dress Islamically? Or can he wear jeans and T-shirts.

ZEYD. Jeans and T-shirts for boys are already Islamic. What is this about? We'll deal with it when the time comes, okay?

AYESHA. See. Having a boy is easier. Won't have to have these arguments.

ZEYD. I don't know why we're arguing, we don't even have a child yet.

(*Under his breath.*) And at this rate we never will.

AYESHA. What if our son or daughter was gay? What then?

ZEYD. Why would you say that?

AYESHA. Like that boy who died. Ahad.

ZEYD. I don't want to talk about this any more.

ZEYD finally pulls away and gives up on the possibility of sex. AYESHA *is on the war path.*

AYESHA. How about his funeral. Would you go to our son's funeral? Would you even give him a funeral? Or would you send him to Freddy's?

ZEYD. You told him no! You sent him to Freddy's!

AYESHA. I made a mistake.

ZEYD. You made a business decision. The right one.

AYESHA. Would you give your son a funeral?

ZEYD. He isn't even born yet and you're planning his funeral.

AYESHA. We're funeral directors. We plan funerals like we eat breakfast, alright, so don't give me that.

Beat.

Well, would you? Or would you disown him?

Long pause.

ZEYD. Do you remember when we first met. I'd just got this job. Thought I was a big man, got my licence, driving around in the hearse, trying to impress you. And I swear, even then I knew. I wanted to marry you. And I promised, promised I would do everything, fucking everything, I could, to make you happy. Because I loved, love you.

Beat.

Now, if I had a son or daughter, and I loved them even half as much as I love you, gay or not gay, hijab or no hijab, teenage pregnancy or not, sin or no sin, I swear to Allah, I will love them.

AYESHA. But that boy –

ZEYD. He isn't my son. That's the reputation of our business in this community. Your mother's legacy. Our livelihood. And if that boy came in tomorrow, crying about his friend, I would do exactly what we did all over again.

AYESHA. And break the law again?

ZEYD. It's their law, not ours. Our law is Allah's law.

AYESHA. And will Allah pay our legal bill now?

ZEYD. The imam is organising a collection for our legal fees.
So yes. Allah will.

Pause. The phone rings. AYESHA *answers.*

AYESHA. Asalamualaikum, Al-Asr Funerals.

Pause.

Yes I'm the funeral director here.

Pause.

Where did you hear that?

Pause.

I see.

Pause.

No I'm not confirming it.

Pause.

No I'm not denying it either.

Pause.

Yes I suppose that means I have no comment at this time.

She hangs up the phone, pale.

ZEYD. Who was that?

AYESHA. *Chronicle.*

ZEYD. About the case? How'd they find out?

AYESHA. They wouldn't say.

ZEYD. What did they say?

AYESHA. Not much.

ZEYD. They'll make us villains.

AYESHA. You don't know that.

ZEYD. When have we ever been the good guys? Never.

AYESHA. Don't let this upset you.

ZEYD. I'm not upset.

AYESHA. Yes you are.

ZEYD. No I'm angry. This is going to be us and them, again. Britishness, Englishness, integration.

AYESHA. We should apologise.

ZEYD (*shouting*). We can't apologise!

(*Quieter*.) Don't you understand? It's out now. The press know. Everyone will know. You think our clients will come back to us if we accept we were wrong? And now Freddy's thinks he can do Muslim funerals, we'll lose business!

AYESHA. Whose fault is that then.

ZEYD. How was I meant to know this would happen?

AYESHA. Look, they won't go to Freddy's over us…

ZEYD. We are a MUSLIM funeral home. I have three numbers on my speed dial. You. My mum. And the imam. We bury the dead. We bury their sinning dead, and we wash them, cleanse them. With our own hands. So our hands need to be clean. We can't be in bed with the kuffar, don't you understand?

AYESHA. We can't afford to lose this case.

ZEYD. We can't afford to apologise! Why didn't you ask Janey? She was always hanging around you back then. I don't understand why you won't speak to her?

AYESHA. She's a human-rights lawyer. She'll side with him.

ZEYD. But what about our human rights! The right to say no? Because it's against our beliefs, our religion? Doesn't matter what they say, homosexuality is a sin, Ayesha, and you know it. And that's how our community will see it.

AYESHA. But you said /

ZEYD. In our heart, we should remember what's wrong and what's right.

Lights down.

Scene Three

In the funeral home. ZEYD is in the front room on a laptop, while AYESHA is in the back room folding some towels and putting them away.

AYESHA. Aren't you meant to be at a janaza this afternoon?

ZEYD. Asked Hamza to do it.

AYESHA. What? Why?

ZEYD. Didn't feel like it.

> *A disapproving pause. AYESHA comes out to the front room.*

AYESHA. You should get off that. It's a waste of time.

ZEYD. Have you seen what they're saying?

AYESHA. No, we have work to do.

> *Beat.*
>
> Your parents rang. Wondering if we'll be coming round for dinner this weekend?

ZEYD. There's a petition to get us shut down.

AYESHA. They're worried about us. About you.

ZEYD. Tell them we're fine.

AYESHA. You could tell them yourself.

> *Beat.*
>
> Mona's grandfather's died.

ZEYD. Look at this: 'This case once again highlights how Muslims are failing to integrate into British culture and I hope the result will uphold British values of equality and democracy.' – this is our fucking MP talking. I'm British too. What about my values?

AYESHA. I need you to collect the body. Mona's grandfather?

ZEYD. Newspaper's saying some Muslims have put up stickers round the area too. Saying homosexuality is a sin and that.

AYESHA. Are you listening? He's at the hospital. Can you go?
This afternoon?

ZEYD. It's a mess. Everything's a mess.

AYESHA. ZEYD!

ZEYD. Yeah yeah. Collection from the hospital.

*Satisfied he's got the message, but shaking her head
frustratedly,* AYESHA *moves back into the back room, but*
ZEYD *follows her, ranting.*

Why was he even in here thinking we'd help? Do you think
it's a set-up? *Daily Mail* or something. Heartless Muslims,
homophobic Muslims. Turn away grieving gay boyfriend.
They always want to give us a bad name.

Beat.

Now that we've been in the paper, I bet loads of them will
come in here, wanting us to do their funerals.

AYESHA. Please will you forget that nonsense and be at least
slightly useful?

ZEYD. You didn't come to bed last night.

Beat.

AYESHA. I was doing some work and fell asleep down here.

The door opens and JANEY *enters.* ZEYD *peeks out.*

ZEYD. Here we go, look, it's already started.

AYESHA. What?

JANEY. Hello?

ZEYD *steps out into the front room.*

ZEYD. Come right in, love, we're a Muslim funeral directors',
but we don't discriminate. We accept all races, faiths,
colours, creeds, genders, sexualities. Come right in, I'll make
you a cuppa.

JANEY. Uh, is Ayesha here?

AYESHA *steps out too.*

ZEYD. I can help you. We do all kinds of funerals, like I said, we don't discriminate.

AYESHA. Zeyd...

ZEYD. If a rhinoceros walked through that door, we'd do a rhinoceros funeral.

AYESHA. It's Janey? Remember her?

ZEYD. Oh. You changed your hair. Looks – nice.

JANEY. Thanks. Your beard filled out alright too.

ZEYD (*touching his beard confused and self-conscious*). What?

AYESHA. What are you doing here?

JANEY. I wanted to speak to you.

ZEYD. Actually we wanted to speak to you too. You're a lawyer right?

JANEY. Yes.

ZEYD. Well, I don't know if Ayesha's told you, but we're involved in this court case.

JANEY *looks to* AYESHA, *confused.* AYESHA *looks to the floor.*

Or maybe you saw it in the paper?

AYESHA. Zeyd...

JANEY. Yes I did.

ZEYD. Anyway, we were wondering if we could ask for your advice on it?

There is a long awkward silence.

Because it's freedom of religion, isn't it? That's our human right, right?

JANEY. Your freedom of religion extends only so far as it doesn't trample the rights of others.

Silence.

AYESHA. Zeyd, why don't you collect Mr Khan. I'll speak to Janey.

ZEYD, *first indignant then disappointed, leaves.*

Sorry.

Beat.

JANEY. How've you been?

AYESHA. Fine.

JANEY. I've seen your case in the papers. Seems to be causing quite the stir.

AYESHA. Yeah – I'm trying not to read it. But we're getting hate mail, phone calls, all kinds of shit.

JANEY. I'm sorry.

AYESHA. It's okay, I'm still alright, but Zeyd's taking it pretty badly.

JANEY. I'm leaving.

AYESHA (*shocked*). What?

JANEY. Mum's better. But we're fighting all the time. Over everything. *The Archers.* The *Ten O'Clock News.* The difference between organic and free-range eggs.

AYESHA. Oh.

JANEY. Being back here. It feels like home, but not, you know? Like I'm a foreigner in the place I was born. You know what I mean?

AYESHA. I can imagine, yeah.

She's a British Muslim – of course she knows what JANEY *means.*

JANEY. And I miss London. It just sucks you in. I was a Londoner from the second I got on the Tube to go to work on my first day. My head in someone's armpit.

Beat.

And I don't know what it does to you, but you start to think
the whole world is like that. A melting pot of cultures, unified
by suits and mobile phones, commuter woes and house-price
grievances. And you know that falafel is Palestinian, and your
Muslim mates can only eat halal meat, but can also go to that
kosher place up in St John's Wood. And you feel like you've
got super powers, like you've cracked it, and the answer to
war and hate, racism and homophobia, and the clash of
civilisations is just to become a Londoner.

Beat.

And now I'm back here and it's home, but it's like – a – a –
twilight zone, like suspended in space and time. The same
prejudices, the same divisions the same small-minded
small-town backwardness that I'd hoped I'd left behind.

AYESHA. Well. If your mum's all well and fine now, you really
have no reason to stay amongst us 'small minded, small-town,
backward' people.

The air is thick with hurt.

JANEY. I didn't speak to her for years you know? After I told
her I was a lesbian.

Pause – this lands with AYESHA.

I came out first year of uni, and she – well she refused to
believe it, refused to accept it. She wanted the big white
wedding, the son-in-law, the grandchildren. She was
embarrassed. Didn't want me to tell Dad either, as if he
would blame her parenting. Like he had any right to given
he'd abdicated all parenting responsibility.

Beat.

And when I brought my girlfriend home, she kept asking what
'my friend would like for tea' or where 'my friend' would like
to visit. And then Mum had the gall to ask her – in front of me
– if she had any nice men in her life. And when my lovely
polite girlfriend, said no, you know what my mum said?

Beat.

'Shame. You're such a pretty girl.'

Beat.

So I decided I wouldn't come back. Teach her a lesson for her homophobia. I'd make her miss me. And well, she really didn't seem to miss me at all.

Beat.

I don't know what I was hoping for.

AYESHA. Why are you telling me this?

JANEY. She stopped me hanging around you because she was afraid I was a lesbian. And I was too weak, too miserable, too ashamed really, to argue with her.

AYESHA. That isn't what she told me.

JANEY. No of course not. She would never have uttered the word out loud. Lesbian. She told me she spun some yarn about me having to study for boarding school.

AYESHA *scoffs.*

Was that not true?

AYESHA. She said you were being bullied because you were only hanging out with me. And she wanted you to spend time with girls you had more in common with. Who shared 'similar upbringings'.

JANEY. God.

Beat.

I didn't realise…

AYESHA. No, you wouldn't.

JANEY. Ayesha, I'm so sorry.

AYESHA. Anyway, you've left once before, you're going to leave again now. And we're talking about eleven years ago. So, it doesn't really matter any more.

JANEY. It DOES matter. What happened then matters. Don't you remember what it was like?

AYESHA (*shrugs*). It wasn't that bad.

JANEY. Wasn't that bad? Ayesha, I couldn't pick up the phone at home if it rang because I was scared. We were so bullied and the school did nothing. NOTHING. People were taught that it was okay to hate us, and we in turn were taught to hate ourselves.

Beat.

Those scars run so deep. I can still feel them today.

Beat.

I'm sorry. I'm so sorry my mum said what she did. I had no idea she made it about – that. Because really, it was never about you, it was always about me. She was terrified, absolutely terrified that the bullying was – justified. That we were a couple and those rumours were true.

Loaded pause.

AYESHA. We were just friends.

JANEY *scoffs*.

At least you got to leave.

Beat.

Did you think about what things were like for me after you left?

JANEY. Of course I did.

AYESHA. Not enough to visit. To call.

Beat.

JANEY. I thought it'd be easier.

AYESHA. Easier for who?

Beat.

You know I ordered a prospectus? For your school. I'd never even heard the word prospectus before then.

Beat.

It looked so amazing, those old brick buildings and big green gardens, all the girls in blazers and ties and soft floppy pony tails. I could see you there. You fit right in. But me.

Shakes her head – 'no'.

Every night I'd lie in bed wishing [I could be with you]. Wishing I could afford to be at that school. Wishing Mum could afford the thousands, tens of thousands of pounds it took to be there.

Beat.

I imagined getting the train down, with my suitcase and uniform. And meeting you there on the platform. Imagined the look on your face. I thought, soon as we were out of this shithole, away from St Marks, away from your mum, things could just go back to normal between you and me.

Beat.

Stupid, wasn't I. To think that. Someone like me in a school like that.

JANEY. You had every right to be there /

AYESHA. Rights. What good are they for someone like me. What am I meant to do with my rights? Where can I go? Rights.

You know, I really wonder how you manage to stand up for anyone in court because you could never stand up for me. You were my best friend and you broke my heart.

Pause.

JANEY. I might have a potential defence. For your case.

AYESHA. A defence?

JANEY. Well, there's actually no defence for turning someone away on the basis of sexuality. You know that, right? Legally speaking, I mean. And morally too in my books. There is one other card you can play though.

AYESHA. What?

JANEY. You could say you turned him away because it was a suicide. Suicide is haram too isn't it? In Islam.

AYESHA. Yes.

JANEY. Suicide isn't a protected characteristic like sexuality. So it wouldn't have been discriminatory in legal terms. You're allowed to discriminate against someone who kills themself. As mad as that is.

AYESHA. I see.

JANEY. And if it seemed odd and the family weren't involved, it might make sense that you turned him away on that basis rather than sexuality. Especially if he didn't make his sexuality explicit.

AYESHA. You think we could win with that argument?

JANEY. Well, not win, but it might just be enough to persuade him to settle out of court. But it really is truly horrendous. To turn someone away in the first place. And then this. But there you go. Your choice.

AYESHA. Why are you helping me now?

JANEY. Why do you think?

Beat.

It was never just friendship for me. I came here because I needed you to know who I am before I left. Who I always was. How I always felt.

Beat.

I was so in love with you.

JANEY *kisses* AYESHA.

Take care, Ayesha.

AYESHA. Janey. Wait. I don't know what to do.

JANEY. I think you've decided already.

JANEY *leaves*.

Lights down.

ACT THREE

Scene One

AYESHA *has come to meet* TOM *on a park bench.*

AYESHA. Thanks for meeting me.

> *Beat –* TOM *is silent.*

I asked to meet you because I wanted to apologise.

TOM. Took your time.

AYESHA. I was waiting for the right moment.

TOM. Four months after he died?

AYESHA. I'm sorry.

TOM. Well. Apology not accepted.

AYESHA. I know.

TOM. What you did. Disgusting.

AYESHA. I know.

TOM. Apologise. What good will that do. None. Nothing. Nothing.

> TOM *lifts his cup to his mouth but it shakes uncontrollably in his tremoring hands. He gives up, puts it down without taking a sip.*

> AYESHA *notices this, proceeds more kindly, more honestly than we have ever heard her speak before.*

AYESHA. You must be in a lot of pain.

TOM. You think?

AYESHA. It's rare that we get in anyone as young as you and your – your friend.

TOM. Boyfriend.

AYESHA. Boyfriend. Most people. They're either older, or they were sick for some time. They're expecting death, you know. It's a bit easier that way maybe.

Beat.

But sometimes, we get the heart attacks, or the car crashes – the ones when you don't expect them. They're different.

Beat.

It's not just grief is it. It's – it's something else.

Beat.

TOM. Is that it? Is that your apology done?

Beat.

Or did you expect me to forgive you?

Pause.

AYESHA. I don't think I'll ever be able to forgive myself.

TOM. You know the irony of it all? He would have forgiven you. I never will, but he would have.

He laughs.

That's the kind of person he was. Better than you. Better than all of us.

Beat.

You know, a few weeks before he died, I came home from work and found him at home with this old man. I mean, the man must have been about eighty at least. And Ahad had come across him, just wandering around on the street crying. He was confused, there was something wrong with him, his mind. Not all there. Talking nonsense, sometimes even shouting. And anyone else would have walked a circle round him. But Ahad – Ahad brought him home. Gave him a cup of tea, some toast. Tried to find out who he was, where he lived. And it turned out his wife had just died, but he didn't know

who to call, or what to do. He just looked so – lost.
Hopeless. Like he wished he'd died with her.

Beat.

That's the kind of man Ahad was. The man you refused to
wash, to bury.

AYESHA. What we did /

TOM. What you did should have been condemned in a court of
law. It should never have turned into some nonsense
despicable legal game, hidden away and settled out of court.
It should have been public. For everyone to see – wrong and
right. What you did was wrong.

AYESHA. I want to make things right. As best I can.

TOM. It's too late. He left me. How can anything ever, ever be
right again.

Voice breaks.

Time fucking heals. Time only numbs if you're lucky.

AYESHA *rummages in her bag and brings out a notepad.
She opens it on a page and hands it to* TOM.

What is this?

AYESHA. I'm going to send it to the local paper. With your
blessing.

TOM *glances at it.*

TOM. Read it.

AYESHA *is hesitant.*

Go on. Read it out. I want to hear you say it.

AYESHA *takes the sheet of paper.*

AYESHA. It uh says. It says: 'We are deeply sorry for our
mistake and the pain we have caused. We would like to make
it clear that Al-Asr Funerals is open to any and all members
of the community.'

TOM. The case is all settled. Why now?

AYESHA. Atonement.

TOM. Bit short isn't it, for atonement. Let's see it again.

AYESHA *hands the pad over.*

Got a pen?

AYESHA *fishes a pen out of her bag.* TOM *gets to work on the sheet of paper, crossing things out, adding things in. When he's done, he slides it back to her.*

AYESHA. 'We deeply regret our decision to refuse a funeral for Mr Ahad Ilyas on the basis of his sexuality, and we are sorry for the pain we have caused his partner Thomas Gibbs.'

Beat.

His family won't want him to be named like this.

TOM. They abandoned him, so their opinion no longer counts. Carry on.

AYESHA. 'We would like to make it clear that Al-Asr Funerals is open to any and all members of the community irrespective of sexuality.'

TOM. There's more.

AYESHA. 'Furthermore, we urge the Muslim community to practice tolerance and acceptance of the LGBTQ' – what's Q for?

TOM. Queer.

AYESHA. 'LGBT – Q – Community.'

Beat.

This is what you want?

TOM. Yes.

AYESHA. We can't say this.

TOM. Well then. We're done here.

AYESHA. Please. This case has riled the community enough. I can offer an apology, just about, but tell them to accept it? Never. They'll never see it as anything but a sin.

TOM. Ahad used to say that the God – the Allah – he believes in, would never create him this way, make him love in the only way he knew how, only to condemn it. That would be a cruel God, and his Allah wasn't cruel.

He'd made peace with it. With Islam.

And he thought, in time, others – other Muslims – would too.

AYESHA. You don't understand this community.

TOM. This community killed my boyfriend!

A silence.

And that should never happen again. Ever. To anyone.

AYESHA. Okay. Okay I will.

TOM. Okay.

TOM *turns away from* AYESHA. *He's done with her. But she continues to sit beside him for some moments in silence.*

AYESHA. There's a prayer in Islam which we say when someone dies: Inna lillahi wa inna ilayhi raji'un. To Allah we all belong and to Allah we all return. It helps me. Sometimes.

TOM. Thank you.

AYESHA. He must have been very brave. To leave his family. Be with you.

This is the first time TOM *begins to soften.*

TOM. Yeah he was.

AYESHA. Did he tell them the truth? About you?

TOM (*nods*). He was a terrible liar, so he had no choice really. And he thought that the world was a good place. He really believed that. How many people do you know like that? That actually think this world is a good fucking benevolent place?

Who can see kindness in the most wretched evil fucking
people.

Beat.

He really believed they'd accept him eventually. And he
waited and he waited, until – I guess he couldn't wait
any more.

AYESHA. Did his family come to the funeral?

TOM. Just his sister. She was always okay with him. Sort of.
She says her parents want to meet me now. It's changed them
apparently.

Beat.

I meet his sister sometimes though. It's nice, we talk
about him.

AYESHA. Does it help?

TOM. I'm scared to stop talking about him.

AYESHA. Tell me about him then.

Pause.

TOM. He fucking loved Bollywood, that man. The dances, the
drama, the moustaches, and saris, but the songs especially.
He'd sing them sometimes. I'd wake up to it some days.
Smell of coffee from the kitchen, and the sound of him
singing away. Wish I'd recorded it now.

Beat.

I wish I had appreciated every second of every day with him.
He was my world.

TOM *collects himself, makes to leave.*

Thanks for – that. The statement.

AYESHA. My husband won't like it. But – if it makes
a difference.

TOM. You know. Ahad thought that the only way to change
people's minds – to make them value love over religion –

was to make them realise we're just like them. If enough daughters and sons and brothers and sisters and husbands and wives came out, they'd have to accept us eventually.

Beat.

But it meant an army of the afraid standing up, and coming out. And as far as he could see in this town, it was just him, just him alone.

Beat – maybe TOM *touches her hand.*

We all need to be brave sometimes, Ayesha. Or else, nothing will ever change.

TOM *leaves.*

Lights down.

Scene Two

At the funeral directors'. AYESHA *is alone, praying.*

ZEYD *crashes in noisily, sees her, glowers, but says nothing as* AYESHA *continues to pray.*

AYESHA *ends her prayer, folds her prayer mat, and drapes it on the end of the sofa.*

ZEYD, *annoyed, picks it up and folds it away in its place.*

ZEYD. Ibrahim's coming over to help with his dad's ghusl.

AYESHA. Okay.

ZEYD. Are you ready?

AYESHA. Yes.

ZEYD. Did you get the green form?

AYESHA. Yes.

ZEYD. Where is it?

AYESHA. Where they usually are.

ZEYD. Well who knows what other big changes you might decide to make without consulting me.

AYESHA. Do you want a cuppa?

ZEYD. No.

AYESHA *clicks the kettle on.*

ZEYD *disappears into the back room.*

ZEYD *removes some towels from a shelf and lays them on the side.*

AYESHA *sits on the sofa with a sigh.* ZEYD *peeps out to look at her. She has her eyes shut.*

(*Gruffly.*) What's wrong with you?

AYESHA. Headache.

ZEYD. You don't need to stay.

The kettle clicks off. AYESHA *pours herself a cup of tea.*

AYESHA. What about for the janaza?

ZEYD. You don't have to come.

AYESHA. Sure?

ZEYD (*shrugs*). I asked Hamza to help.

His phone beeps and he reads the text.

Ibrahim's on Asian time anyway. Why don't you go upstairs, lie down.

AYESHA. Okay.

AYESHA *gets up to go.*

ZEYD. We made the money back.

AYESHA. What?

ZEYD. With this last one. We can pay the mosque back what we borrowed. For the settlement.

AYESHA. That's good.

ZEYD. Like it never happened.

AYESHA. Right.

ZEYD. I wish it never happened.

AYESHA. I know.

ZEYD. I wish you'd never done what you did. Apologised. To that kuffar.

Beat.

I'll never understand why, Ayesha.

Beat.

What's done is done. At least we can move on now. Get back on track.

AYESHA *sits back down.*

AYESHA. I don't know if I can.

ZEYD. What do you mean?

AYESHA. I don't know if I want to keep doing this.

ZEYD. I could do it. You could take some time out. Do a – uni course if you wanted. Hamza's tired of the garage and looking for a change. He thinks his wife might help out here too, with the female ghusls and all, if you show her the ropes.

AYESHA. You're not listening to me.

ZEYD. We can get past this. I know I've been a bit tough on you. About what you did, publishing that – stuff – in the paper.

AYESHA. I've told you /

ZEYD. Well it wasn't you who had to explain it to the imam, to clients, to my parents!

AYESHA. I would if you /

ZEYD. What and made it worse?

AYESHA. We can't keep having this argument.

ZEYD. Sorry. I'm just – it's like you sided with that kuffar over me.

AYESHA. Do you really think that?

ZEYD. Yes.

AYESHA. That he's a kuffar?

Beat – AYESHA *has tangentially agreed she sided with* TOM. *This lands with* ZEYD.

ZEYD. It's haram, Ayesha. What don't you understand about that?

Pause. AYESHA *hardens.*

AYESHA. I've been thinking of selling this place.

ZEYD. What? You can't do that.

AYESHA. Why not? I'm the registered company director, not you.

ZEYD. You can't sell this place – it's, it's all we know. And it's where I met you, and –

AYESHA. I can't be here any more.

ZEYD. Who will run it then?

AYESHA. Well, as the imam seems to have so many opinions on running this place, maybe he should do it.

ZEYD. What about me?

AYESHA. You were the one saying pack it all in anyway? Just a few months ago. You wanted us to quit this, look to the future, remember? So let's do it. I'll sell it. We'll close up shop, and – I don't know, let's go travelling.

ZEYD. I was saying that because I wanted to make you happy. And because living without death staring us in the face every single day, might have helped us, helped our relationship.

But you – you want to give it all up for what? Because of that kuffar? Not for me, that's for sure.

Beat.

Do you even love me at all?

AYESHA. What?

ZEYD. Things are so – fucked with us, lately. I've never felt so alone.

AYESHA. Don't say that.

ZEYD. It's the truth. Do you know what it feels like? To love someone so much. And for them to feel nothing for you. Nothing.

Beat.

And don't tell me it's not true, because I know, I can feel it. And everything I do, everything I tried to do, to be a good husband to you – nothing works, I just can't win you. Day after day, hour after hour, night after night of lying next to you, afraid, afraid to touch you. Afraid to touch my wife, because I know you don't want me to.

Beat.

Look at me, I'm not even a man any more. It's pathetic. I'm so desperate, so fucking tired of it all, it feels like my whole body's just been minced up in a meat grinder.

Beat.

Well say something.

AYESHA. I'm sorry.

ZEYD. What have I done? What can I do? Why won't I ever be good enough for you?

AYESHA. It's not you.

ZEYD. Oh 'it's not you, it's me' right?

AYESHA. Yes.

ZEYD *sits, broken.*

It's not you.

I just thought it would be a secret I'd have to die with. And if I don't tell you now – I think it'll be what kills me.

Beat.

I'm a lesbian.

ZEYD. What are you talking about?

AYESHA. I think I've always known. In my heart.

ZEYD. No, you're wrong. You're not.

AYESHA. Yes, Zeyd. I am.

ZEYD. It's – it's haram.

AYESHA. Maybe. But it's all I know.

ZEYD. You married me! You said you wanted to marry me! I don't believe it.

AYESHA. I tried not to believe it, either.

ZEYD. Well try harder, that's not fucking good enough. Is that what you'll say? Say to your maker, on the Day of Judgement? I tried? Is that it?

AYESHA. The Allah I believe in. He's good. He's kind. Isn't he? He wouldn't make me like this, love like this, only to condemn it. To make these feelings I have – I have always had – to make them a sin. That would be a cruel god, Zeyd. And my Allah is not cruel.

ZEYD. What am I going to tell my parents? Our friends?

AYESHA. Whatever you like. The truth?

ZEYD. Hah! Is it her? Janey? She brainwashed you or something? She was obsessed with you even then, don't you see it?

AYESHA. It has always been there. Before Janey. After Janey. She just opened the door and asked me to walk through it. But it has always been there, in me.

ZEYD. What does it feel like?

Pause.

AYESHA. Like a fire raging through me, screaming, just
screaming to get out.

Beat.

Look at you, Zeyd. Look at you. Look at what it's done to
you. Look at what I have done to you. This case, and the
man it's made you become, so full of hate.

Beat.

I was bullied you know. Called names. The girls at school
knew it about me. And I think you know too.

ZEYD. No.

AYESHA. You hate that poor gora boy because you know. It's
not like you, to spout so much hate. You're not that person.
You're a good person, Zeyd, I know you. I see how you
speak to people when they're grieving. When they're broken.
You're gentle and understanding. You don't judge. You take
care of people. I know you. You want your daughter to be a
politician. You washed my mother's mangled body so I
didn't have to. You hold strangers' hands and rub their backs
while they cry. I know you. And I can see what I've done to
you. How I've turned you into this. Because I know, in your
heart you knew. You knew who I was, what I am.

Beat.

I'm sorry, Zeyd, I'm sorry. Forgive me?

ZEYD (*crying*). But I love you.

AYESHA. I love you too.

Beat.

But I can't do this to you any more. To us. Look at us. We
can't live like this any more, Zeyd, we just can't.

Beat.

ZEYD. What about the business?

AYESHA. You can have it. It's yours. You've always found it so easy, so natural.

ZEYD. And you?

AYESHA. You think I wanted to run this place? I hate it, Zeyd, I hate it. I have always hated it.

ZEYD. What about me? Us?

AYESHA. We'll be fine, my love. We'll be fine.

AYESHA *hugs a sobbing* ZEYD.

[ZEYD *pulls away.*]

[ZEYD. Ibrahim will be here soon. I'm gonna...]

[ZEYD *wipes his eyes. Exits, leaving* AYESHA *alone.*]

Scene Three

AYESHA *is packing the funeral home up into boxes. As she works, she sings 'Madhaniya' – a Punjabi folk song traditionally sung by women at mehndi nights.*

JANEY *appears towards the end, holding two cups of tea, but* AYESHA *doesn't notice and continues to sing absent-mindedly before fading out.*

JANEY. Don't stop now.

AYESHA *jumps, startled.*

AYESHA. I thought I was alone.

JANEY. Sorry. You left the door open. I like the song though. Not quite the serenade I was expecting, but not bad.

AYESHA. It's quite apt actually. It's about a bride leaving her family home to go off and get married.

JANEY. Steady on. It's only a cup of tea.

JANEY hands her a tea. AYESHA laughs.

AYESHA. Thanks.

JANEY sits beside AYESHA.

JANEY. You nearly done here?

AYESHA looks around the home.

AYESHA. Yes.

Looks at JANEY, perhaps even takes her hand, and smiles.

I think so.

Lights down. 'Madhaniya' plays over.

End.

A Nick Hern Book

The Funeral Director first published in Great Britain as a paperback original in 2018 by Nick Hern Books Limited, The Glasshouse, 49a Goldhawk Road, London W12 8QP, in association with Papatango Theatre Company

The Funeral Director copyright © 2018 Iman Qureshi

Iman Qureshi has asserted her right to be identified as the author of this work

Cover image: Rebecca Pitt; photography by Michael Wharley

Designed and typeset by Nick Hern Books, London
Printed in Great Britain by Mimeo Ltd, Huntingdon, Cambridgeshire PE29 6XX

A CIP catalogue record for this book is available from the British Library

ISBN 978 1 84842 796 9

Woodland
CARBON
www.woodlandcarbon.co.uk
NICK HERN BOOKS
Printed on Carbon Captured paper